Projects Inspired by 20th Ce

Claire Tinker

Acknowledgements

The author and publishers would like to thank the children of Hunters Bar and Nook Lane Junior schools for once again rising to every artistic challenge and producing such inspirational and superb works of art.

A big thank you to head teachers Gina and Jill and to all staff for their continuing encouragement and support and especially to Claire Scott for all her generous help and artistic eye.

Finally, last but not least, a big thank you to all my family and friends who have been as enthusiastic and excited about this book as I have.

Demkin Display (page 45)

Published by Collins, An imprint of HarperCollins*Publishers*
77 – 85 Fulham Palace Road, Hammersmith, London, W6 8JB

Browse the complete Collins catalogue at
www.collinseducation.com

© HarperCollins*Publishers* Limited 2011
Previously published in 2006 by Folens as 'A Century of Art'
First published in 2006 by Belair Publications

10 9 8 7 6 5 4 3 2 1

ISBN-13 978-0-00-743945-4

Claire Tinker asserts her moral rights to be identified as the author of this work

British Library Cataloguing in Publication Data
A Catalogue record for this publication is available from the British Library

Every effort has been made to trace copyright holders and to obtain their permission for the use of copyright material. The authors and publishers will gladly receive any information enabling them to rectify any error or omission in subsequent editions.

Commissioning Editor: Zöe Nichols   Editors: Sara Wiegand
Cover design: Mount Deluxe   Page layout: Suzanne Ward
Photography: RB Photography and Steve Forest

Printed and bound by Printing Express Limited, Hong Kong

Mixed Sources
Product group from well-managed forests and other controlled sources
www.fsc.org Cert no. SW-COC-001806
© 1996 Forest Stewardship Council
FSC

Contents

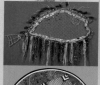
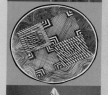

Introduction

The art of the twentieth century was characterised by enormous richness and complexities. It was one of the most dynamic and exciting periods of art history, a time of radical change and development as artists challenged established assumptions and ideas.

During the twentieth century, artists began to experiment with new styles and techniques and gathered in groups to discuss ideas. Individuals with similar aims and beliefs often joined together to form a movement. Each movement was deliberately created to make a point. Apart from instilling the artists with a sense of solidarity and confidence, each movement provided a platform to proclaim concepts and gain authority. Groups of artists tended to be taken more seriously than individuals.

This book is intended as a broad-ranging and loosely chronological introduction to some of the most important developments in art and design during the twentieth century. It is by no means comprehensive or a definitive linear history of art movements; to attempt to do so would be misleading and distorting. The movements were seldom self-contained or simply defined. Often they were complicated, contradictory and overlapping. Selections in each chapter have been a personal choice.

Some artists would openly claim to be part of a movement; for others, classifying their work into a particular 'ism' would be open to debate, as the boundaries are fluid and not always observed or defined by the artists themselves. It can be tempting to pigeon-hole artists according to a movement, but it should be remembered that some of the most famous artists of the twentieth century moved in and out of many movements or simply transcended them; each artist is an individual and every work of art unique.

Each chapter in this book, in roughly chronological order, represents an art movement of the twentieth century. Most begin with an example of work by an artist closely linked to that particular movement, followed by an activity using the featured artwork as a starting stimulus. The other activities in each chapter are linked to additional artists within the movement and examples of their work can easily be found on the internet. Each chapter contains a brief introduction to the movement, information about various artists and suggestions on how the children can be encouraged to engage and respond to the concepts and ideology within the movement. The resulting displays aim to further your children's understanding of modern art, whilst also making a valuable aesthetic contribution to your school environment.

Twentieth-century art can appear difficult or even incomprehensible, and the associated vocabulary can be daunting. The aim of this book is to provide teachers with an accessible route into the world of modern art. It offers ideas to present to children, activities to pursue in both two- and three-dimensions and hopefully will generate a fertile ground for artistic exploration and discussion.

Claire Tinker

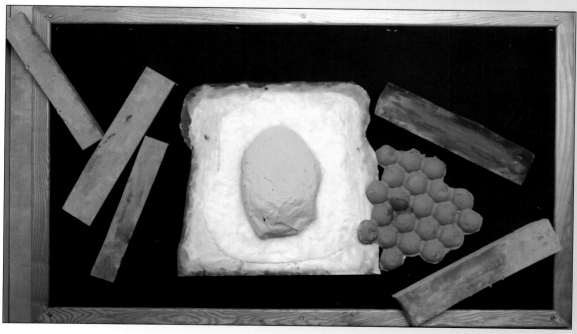

Art Nouveau is a style of decoration, design and architecture of the late 1890s and early 1900s. It was an international movement that swept through Europe and the USA, although Paris and Brussels are regarded by many as the birthplace of Art Nouveau. As the name suggests it was a deliberate attempt to create a new style after the clutter and preoccupation with historical forms of the Victorian era. Its most characteristic themes were lines and motifs based on plant forms, birds, and female figures with abundant flowing hair.

The Kiss by Gustav Klimt (1862–1918) © Corel

Gustav Klimt

Gustav Klimt (1862–1918) was born in Baumgartner near Vienna, Austria. His father was a gold engraver but the family was very poor. Klimt entered the Vienna public art school at the age of 14 and first made his name as a painter and decorator. In 1893 Klimt moved into his own studio and started to paint. He was explicitly erotic and people criticised his work as corrupt and generally didn't understand his symbolism. This painting by Klimt, entitled *The Kiss,* shows the influence of Art Nouveau with its decorative, brightly coloured pattern and swirling shapes.

Klimt Display

Resources
- Card
- Viewfinders
- Collage materials
- Paint and paintbrushes
- Glue
- Scissors
- Fabric
- Plastic mask

Approach

1. Show the children Gustav Klimt's *The Kiss* on page 6. Encourage them to talk about the shapes, patterns, colours and composition of the picture, asking relevant questions to focus the discussion.

2. Provide the children with viewfinders and ask them to select a particularly interesting area of decoration to look at closely.

3. Give each child a piece of card. Refer them to the area highlighted by their viewfinder and discuss how they could develop a similar design on their piece of card.

4. Provide the children with a variety of paint and collage materials to create their own Klimt-style pattern.

5. Use the same technique to paint a Klimt-style figure onto fabric. Embellish the fabric with sequins and gold materials and display with a plastic mask.

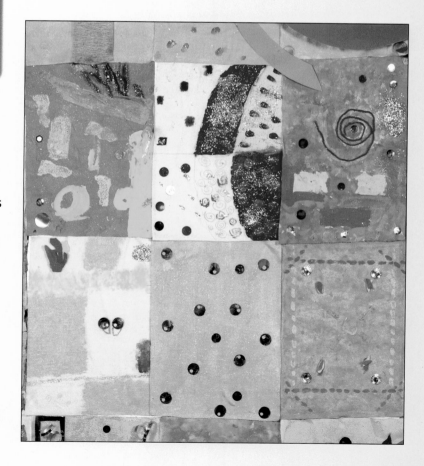

Klimt Photo Frames

Resources
- Examples of paintings by Gustav Klimt
- Pre-made photograph frames
- Paint and paintbrushes
- Glue
- Collage materials

Approach

1. Encourage the children to study and discuss the patterns and swirling designs of the pictures by Gustav Klimt.

2. Ask the children to sketch out some ideas and collect suitable collage materials to decorate their own Klimt photo frame.

3. Decorate the photo frames and challenge the children to draw an appropriate Klimt-style picture to display inside.

Antoni Gaudi

Antoni Gaudi (1852–1926) was a deeply religious man who devoted much of his personal life to designing and building one of the most remarkable cathedrals in the history of architecture; the 'Sagrada Familia' ('The Holy Family') in Barcelona. He was fortunate to have as his patron a rich Spanish intellectual called Count Don Eusebio Guell. Gaudi built him an extraordinary palace in Barcelona, which housed curious pictures and structures made out of mosaic tiles, pieces of marble shards and pottery.

Gaudi Dragon

Approach

1. Show the children pictures of the Art Nouveau style of Gaudi, particularly the mosaic patterns on the dragon fountain in Park Guell.

2. Encourage the children to mould the wire into a dragon shape.

3. Soak the strips of Modroc in water for three to four seconds then cover the wire mesh thoroughly with the plaster bandages.

4. When dry, paint the dragon and then cover it with small square tiles.

Resources
- Examples of Gaudi's mosaics (e.g. the dragon fountain in Park Guell, Barcelona)
- Modroc plaster bandages
- Wire mesh
- Glue
- Pieces of tiles

Louis Comfort Tiffany

Louis Comfort Tiffany (1848–1933) was an American artist and craftsman who owned a glassworks. He experimented with blending colours and inventing new ways of making ornamental glass. He liked to decorate his glassware with shapes based on nature such as insects, flowers and birds.

Tiffany Tree

Resources
- Pictures of Tiffany lamps
- Large sheets of card for the lamp base
- Smaller sheets of card/one per child
- Paint and paintbrushes
- Brown tissue paper
- Glue

Approach

1. Cover the large sheet of card with brown paint. Scrunch up some brown tissue paper and glue it onto the dark brown background to create texture, so that the base looks like the trunk of a tree. Allow to dry.

2. Show the children pictures of Tiffany lamps and ask them to recreate a small part of the pattern, in this case a spray of Tiffany flowers.

3. Mix some paint accordingly and encourage the children to paint their spray of flowers.

4. When dry, ask the children to cut out each of their flower patterns and display all of the flowers together on the tree trunk background, in the shape of a lamp.

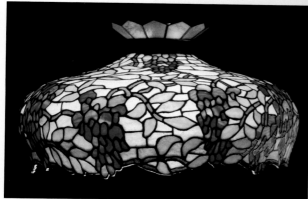

Tiffany lamp © Peter Harholdt/CORBIS

Fauvism

In 1905 an exhibition was held in Paris which included a room full of pictures that blazed with unnatural use of colour, painted with passionate and powerful brushstrokes. One critic called the creators of these paintings 'fauves' (wild beasts) and the name stuck. Fauvism was the first major avant-garde art movement of the twentieth century and it dominated the modern art scene in Europe until 1908 before being overshadowed by a new movement, Cubism. Fauvism was a movement of like-minded artists who rejected the delicate and more subtle style of the Impressionists. Their unnatural colours were fierce and highly contrasting, often deliberately clashing. It was never a consciously organised movement with an agreed agenda, but rather a loose affiliation of artists who shared the same ideas.

Fauvist Fabric Collage

Approach

1. Look at the vibrant and intensely vivid colours of Fauvist portraits, such as this one by André Derain.

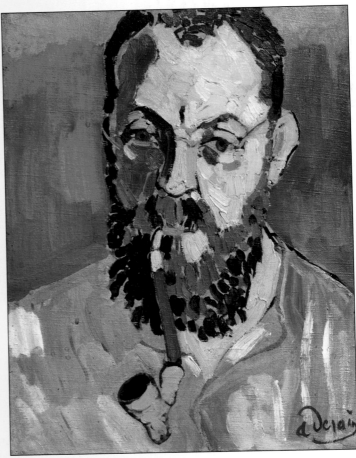

Henri Matisse, 1905 by André Derain (1880–1954)
Image © Tate, London 2006; Artwork © ADAGP, Paris and DACS, London 2006

2. Discuss how Fauvist artists caused scandal with their use of unnatural colours and apparently frenzied brushwork.

3. Ask the children to sketch out a portrait of their partner and talk about possible colours which would give their work the Fauvist shock value.

4. Use a variety of collage materials to produce a fabric Fauvist portrait and display it on a background of tie and die fabric.

Resources
- Examples of Fauvist portraits (e.g. *Portrait of André Derain*, 1905 by Henri Matisse; *Portrait of Matisse*, 1905 by André Derain)
- Pieces of white cloth
- Collage materials
- Glue
- Scissors
- Paper and pencils
- Dye
- Elastic bands

Henri Matisse

Henri Matisse (1869–1954) is widely held to be one of the great masters of twentieth-century art. He was born at la Cateau in France and moved to Paris as a young man to study law, but abandoned it to become an artist in 1891. He was considered the leader of Fauvism, although he never felt tied down to one particular style and continued to experiment throughout his life. Matisse was fascinated by sculpture and during his lifetime made about 70 sculptures. In his seventies illness left him bedridden and he could no longer work at an easel. With the help of assistants he began creating brightly coloured cut-outs which he called 'drawings with scissors'.

Matisse Wallpaper

Resources
- Cartridge paper
- Paint and paintbrushes

Approach

1. Talk to the children about the Fauvist way of painting. Look at Henri Matisse's *Algerian Woman*. Discuss how strong outlines can have a dramatic effect and how unusual colour combinations can have a striking impact.

2. Give the children the opportunity to experiment with designs and colour combinations using paint. Emphasise that the effect will be created by the colour and that the children should not get too particular about detailed design.

3. When the children are happy with their designs, transfer them onto a large sheet of paper, then paint.

4. Discuss how well Fauvist designs work as interior decoration and what type of room they would be suitable for.

5. Display the designs on scrolls as shown.

Colour Wheels and Portraits

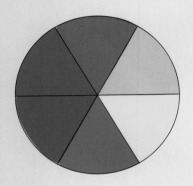

Approach

1. Explain to the children that the colour wheel shows the primary colours (red, yellow and blue) and how they mix with their neighbours to make secondary colours. Complementary colours face each other across the wheel and when placed together they have a strong vibrant effect. The three main pairs of complementary colours are:

   - Red/green
   - Orange/blue
   - Purple/yellow

Resources
- Examples of Fauvist portraits (see page 10)
- Coloured ink
- Paint and paintbrushes
- Paper
- Mirrors

2. Explain to the children how the Fauvists created wild vibrant effects by putting complementary colours together rather than using 'real life' colours.

3. Draw patterns on circular pieces of paper and ask the children to choose a pair of complementary colours to paint the patterns. Discuss the resulting effect.

4. Show the children pictures of Fauvist portraits and explain how their work tended to be joyful. Discuss how the use of colour contributed to this effect.

5. Ask the children to sketch out a portrait of their partner or use mirrors to do a self-portrait.

6. Demonstrate how to paint in the Fauvist style with clashing unexpected colours and crude thick outlines. Allow the children to experiment, using different combinations of colours, before painting their own portrait.

7. Discuss the effect of the colour combinations.

André Derain

André Derain (1880–1954) was born in Chatou, a suburb of Paris. Although his parents hoped he would pursue a career as an engineer or military officer, his main love was to paint along the banks of the Seine or visit the Louvre. Matisse persuaded Derain's parents to support their son's choice of a career and he took up art as a full-time profession. With the outbreak of war Derain joined the military, but returned to Paris in 1919 to continue his work as an artist.

Derain Landscapes

Resources
- Pictures of Derain's landscapes (e.g. *Effect of Sunlight on Water*, 1906; *Charing Cross Bridge*, London, 1906; *Waterloo Bridge*, 1905)
- Paper
- Paint and paintbrushes
- Photographs of local scenes

Approach

1. Show the children a copy of *Waterloo Bridge* by André Derain and point out that this was a painting in which Derain celebrated light. Encourage the children to look at his technique of painting colours and light. Point out how the light explodes and radiates from the sky like a firework display. Introduce other Derain landscapes and discuss his treatment and application of paint in separate blocks of colour, in the Fauvist style.

2. Give the children a brightly coloured photograph of a local scene and ask them to look at it 'through the eyes of Derain', breaking up the colour into closely related tones.

3. Demonstrate how the colour can be mixed and applied in close random strokes and, after the children have practised creating the effect, ask them to compose a Derain-style landscape.

4. Some children could use a copy of the photograph as a base on which to apply paint in the style of Derain.

Around the turn of the century many artists were experimenting with ways to convey their feelings through art. The Expressionists believed art should try to change society and make it less conservative. As the name suggests, Expressionism was all about expressing the artists' inner emotions; its aim was to provoke feelings of discomfort and to challenge the traditional way of looking at the world. The Expressionists were very influenced by the paintings of Edward Munch and Vincent Van Gogh who used vivid colours and exaggerated swirling brushstrokes to give the sense of energy and movement in their work. The movement gathered force in 1905 in Germany where some young artists formed a group called 'Die Brucke' ('The Bridge'). They chose the name because they wanted to forge a bridge to the future with a new kind of art. Key members were Ernst Ludwig Kirchner and Erich Heckler. Another German group of Expressionists were 'Der Blaue Reiter' ('The Blue Rider'), and this group of artists were led by Vassily Kandinsky and Franz Marc. They chose the name purely because Marc liked horses, Kandinsky liked riders and they both liked blue!

In its broadest sense, Expressionism is a term to describe art of any period that is expressive of inner turmoil and deep feelings rather than objective observation and representation.

Ein Warter, 1916 by Erich Heckel (1883–1970) Image © Albright-Knox Art Gallery/ CORBIS; Artwork © VG Bild-Kunst, Bonn and DACS, London 2006

Ernst Ludwig Kirchner

Ernst Ludwig Kirchner (1880–1938) was born in Aschaffenburg near Dresden, Bavaria and is regarded as the leading personality behind the artists' group 'Die Brucke'. The artists of the 'Die Brucke' Expressionists were fascinated and hugely influenced by primitive art. When World War I began, Kirchner signed up for military service but he was discharged only a year later because of a mental breakdown. After World War I, Expressionism became very fashionable in Germany. Sadly this ended in 1933, when Hitler declared all Expressionists as degenerate and 639 of Kirchners' paintings were confiscated; some were sold and others destroyed. This affected Kirchner greatly and he became more and more depressed and committed suicide in 1938.

Arguably some of the best works of the Expressionist movement were produced in the dramatic, bold and graphic medium of the woodcut.

Press Print Portraits

Resources
- Examples of Expressionist woodcuts
- Polystyrene press print sheets
- Paint and paintbrushes
- Cartridge paper

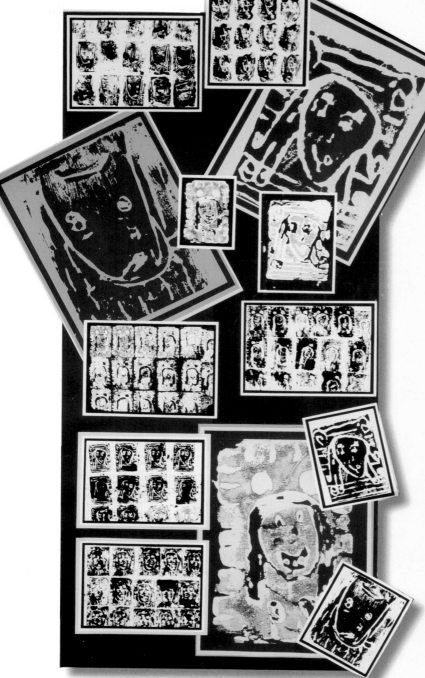

Approach

1. Look at examples of Expressionist woodcuts (for example *Ein Warter* by Erich Heckel on page 14). Discuss how the artist's main focus was to express deep emotions through exaggeration and distortion. Ask the children to 'interpret' the emotions on the faces of the examples provided.

2. Give the children a small piece of cartridge paper and ask them to choose a strong emotion and sketch out an Expressionist portrait.

3. When the children are happy with their portrait, transfer the design onto a polystyrene print sheet using a sharp pencil. Demonstrate the pressure required to achieve a clear print without going through the polystyrene.

4. Apply paint to the print sheet and press it firmly onto a sheet of paper to make a print of the portrait.

5. Repeat the print process as many times as required.

Vincent Van Gogh

Vincent Van Gogh (1853–90) was a key influence behind the Expressionist movement. He inspired a new generation of Expressionist artists who believed the most important thing was self-expression rather than following traditional rules of art.

Van Gogh was born in a small village in Holland. At 27 years old he went to Paris to study art and developed a style that expressed strong emotions through the thick application of paint with broad passionate brushstrokes. Van Gogh was poor all his life and was troubled by attacks of severe depression. Many of his pictures reflect his anxiety and troubled state of mind.

Van Gogh Self-Portraits

Approach

Resources
- Examples of Van Gogh self-portraits (e.g. *Portrait de l'Artiste*, 1889)
- Textured wallpaper with swirling patterns
- Paint and paintbrushes
- Paper and pencils

1. Show the children a Van Gogh self-portrait. Discuss how the swirling shapes in the background give an indication as to the artist's state of mind. Explain how Van Gogh uses various brushwork techniques to create the effects of movement and texture. Look at the choice of colour and the movement of the line; these are clues as to the mood of the self-portrait. Study the expression on Van Gogh's face; discuss how the powerful stare of the eyes explains what is he feeling.

2. Challenge the children to make sketches of different facial expressions. Encourage them to choose a particular feeling that would work well with the textured swirling background paper. This expression could be gloomy, thoughtful, upset or agitated, for example.

3. On a new piece of paper encourage the children to paint individual self-portraits using mirrors or working from their sketches or even photographs.

4. Ask the children to paint their wallpaper background in shades of blue and green.

5. Ask the children to cut out their self-portraits and stick them onto the coloured background. Discuss the effect of the portrait on the background and how this mood could be changed by altering the colour of the background or the shapes and direction of the brushstrokes.

Edvard Munch

The foundations of Expressionism were laid in the 1880s, and Edward Munch (1863–1944) was a major influence on 'Die Brucke' artists. He did not call himself an Expressionist, but his work portrayed moods very strongly and the exaggerated distorted shapes he created express huge emotional storms of anxiety. He was born on a farm in Englehaugh near Loten in Southern Norway and began to study art formally at the age of 17, when he attended the Oslo State School of Art and Handcraft.

The Scream

Resources
- Pictures of Edvard Munch's work (e.g. *The Scream*, 1893)
- Cartridge paper
- Marbling tray
- Marbling ink
- Wax pastels or wax crayons

Approach

1. Look at pictures of *The Scream* by Edvard Munch, one of the world's most famous paintings. Discuss how the landscape is alive with nervous energy; the blood red sky and the swirling lines emphasise the sense of horror and fear. Talk about how it appears to represent the painter's troubled mind as it was executed with energetic and expressive brushstrokes.

2. Ask the children to pull angry, troubled, screaming faces. Encourage them to study and explain how their face changes and how they feel when making these gestures.

3. Ask the children to use wax pastels or crayons to draw a person in the style of Munch, emphasising feelings of anger.

4. Choose two or three marbling colours and demonstrate the process of creating swirling sky conditions by dropping marbling ink into the water and combing it in circular movements.

5. Invite each child to place their wax picture face down on top of the swirling ink. Lift out and leave to dry.

Cubism

Cubism is a style of painting developed in 1908 by Pablo Picasso and Georges Braque and was the first form of Abstract art of the twentieth century. Cubist artists were interested in the way we look at the world and created paintings which showed things from different angles at the same time; they pictured the world as a jigsaw of many sides or faceted solids. The movement was strongly influenced by African sculpture, particularly its sharply faceted surfaces; this influence is seen in early Cubist work, which represents individual form as broken up into jagged angular planes.

Glasses, Newspaper and a Bottle of Wine, circa 1914 by Juan Gris (1887–1927) Image © Burstein Collection/CORBIS

Juan Gris

Juan Gris (1887–1927) was born in Spain but moved to France in 1906 when he was 19. He didn't begin painting seriously until 1910 when he rented a studio close to Picasso in Montmartre. Although Gris did not invent Cubism he was one of its most talented exponents. His immediate surroundings inspired his subject matter and he produced still life compositions of everyday objects.

Still Life Display

Resources

- Examples of Cubist still life pictures (e.g. *Glasses, Newspaper and a Bottle of Wine*, circa 1914, by Juan Gris on page 18)
- Cartridge paper
- Art pencils, charcoal and chalk
- A collection of still life objects
- Collage paper
- Paint and paintbrushes
- Glue

Approach

1. Set up a still life group including objects such as a newspaper, bottles, musical instruments, and so on.

2. Show pictures of Cubist artwork, particularly the three-dimensional collages which use everything from fabric and string to wood and nails.

3. Ask the children to identify the objects in the paintings, noting how all of the objects appear fragmented and unreal.

4. Supply the children with cartridge paper and art pencils and ask them to make a detailed observational sketch of the still life composition.

5. Referring again to the Cubist pictures, ask the children to look at their still life drawing and try to see it in terms of cones, cubes and geometric shapes.

6. Challenge the children to use a variety of different types of textured collage papers to recreate their composition in the style of a Juan Gris still life. Use shapes torn from newspapers, magazines and wrapping paper. Try to put them together in unusual ways.

Pablo Picasso

Pablo Picasso (1881–1973) was born in Malaga, Spain, the son of a painter and an art teacher. From 1900 to 1904 he divided his time between Paris and Barcelona, finally settling in Paris in 1904. He experimented with many different styles. The origin of Cubism is usually linked to Picasso's discovery of so-called 'primitive art', in particular tribal masks. Between 1907 and 1914 he formed a close friendship with Georges Braque, and together they pioneered Cubism. Picasso was a prolific artist and he provided the incentive for many revolutionary changes. It is impossible to confine him to any particular movement as he often worked simultaneously on a wealth and variety of themes, allowing the expression of the subject matter to determine the style.

3D Picasso Cubes

Resources
- Examples of Cubist portraits by Picasso (e.g. *Weeping Woman*, 1937)
- 3D boxes
- Paint and paintbrushes
- Wax pastels
- Glue

Approach

1. Show the children pictures of Picasso's Cubist portraits. Discuss how, by distorting the faces and exaggerating the expressions, he makes the emotions of the portrait immediately apparent.

2. Draw the children's attention to the choice of colour in the portraits. In the *Weeping Woman* in particular the colours are vivid, violent and angry. What effect does this have on the portrait?

3. Cut pieces of paper to fit the faces of the boxes.

4. Give each child a piece of paper and ask them to recreate a Cubist portrait in the style of Picasso. Discuss the emotions they are going to portray and their choice of shapes and colours.

5. Encourage them to paint or colour their design in wax pastels.

6. Glue each design onto the box and display together as Cubist cuboids.

Paul Cézanne

Paul Cézanne (1839–1906) was born in Aix-en-Provence in the south of France. His father was a successful merchant banker. Initially Cézanne studied law but abandoned this career to become a painter, despite the opposition of his father who wanted him to work in the family firm. He had a difficult and complex personality, appeared awkward in Paris café society, and was well-known for his scruffy appearance and rudeness. His work of the 1870s was in an Impressionist style, but he soon decided that he wanted to portray something more 'solid and durable'. In attempting to achieve this he developed a new way of seeing that had a crucial influence on Cubism, exploring the visual and psychological effects of showing things from different angles simultaneously.

Cubist Landscapes

Resources
- Examples of landscapes by Paul Cézanne (e.g. *Le Lac d'Annecy* (*Lake Annecy*), 1896; *Montagnes en Provence* (*Mountains in Provence*), 1886–90)
- Photos and pictures of landscapes
- Paint and paintbrushes
- Glue
- Paper

Approach

1. Show the children pictures of landscapes by Cézanne. Explain that Cézanne built his paintings from blocks of colour. Like pieces in a mosaic, his work often showed things from multiple points of view simultaneously. There are no perspective devices as Cézanne wanted to show three-dimensional spaces in his paintings only by using colour.

2. Give the children a picture of a landscape. Try to analyse the different shapes in the picture and cut up the picture accordingly.

3. Use a mixture of cut paper, painted paper and cut landscape photographs or pictures to create an abstract Cubist landscape with the pieces. Reinforce the Cubist idea that all paintings are made up of cuboid shapes.

The Futurism movement was founded by the poet Filippo Marinetti. Its members, who included Umberto Boccioni, Carlo Carra, Giacomo Balla and Gino Severini, rejected the past and instead celebrated the dynamism of the machine age and city life. The Futurists loved speed, noise pollution, machines and cities and celebrated the most advanced technology of the twentieth century in sculpture and painting. The Futurist movement lasted only a few extraordinary years, beginning with the 1909 publication of the Marinetti Futurist Manifesto and continuing until the end of World War I.

Dynamism of a Dog on a Leash, 1912 by Giacomo Balla (1871–1958) Image © Albright-Knox Art Gallery/CORBIS; Artwork © SIAE, Rome and DACS, London 2006.

Giacomo Balla

Giacomo Balla (1871–1958) was one of the leaders of the Futurist movement. Along with Umberto Boccioni, Carlo Carra and Gino Severini, he signed the first Futurist manifesto in 1910. He was born in Turin and was mainly a self-taught artist. In 1895 he moved to Rome where he spent the rest of his life. Balla was not interested in violence and machines. His paintings tended towards the lyrical and witty and showed the characteristic Futurist aim of portraying motion.

Dog on a Leash

Resources
- Cartridge paper
- Wax pastels or wax crayons
- Paper fasteners

Approach

1. Look at the picture of Giacomo Balla's *Dynamism of a Dog on a Leash* on page 22 and discuss how this group of Futurists was intent on reflecting the aesthetics of the new century, especially speed and power. Discuss whether Balla has been successful in reflecting the dog's movement and if so how this was achieved.

2. Ask the children to choose a picture of any breed of dog to sketch onto a piece of cartridge paper. Once the sketch is complete, cut it out.

3. Show the children how to cut the legs, tail, ears and jaw off the main body of the dog and re-attach the pieces using paper fasteners. It should now be possible to move these parts around. Stick down the main body onto paper, taking care not to glue the moveable parts.

4. Demonstrate how to place the leg in one position and use a wax pastel or crayon to shade around it. Move the leg slightly and shade again. Do this several times and repeat the process for the tail, ears and jaw. The finished composition should look as if the dog is moving.

Street Light

Resources
- Pictures of *Street Light* by Giacomo Balla
- Black card
- Coloured crayons
- Silk
- Silk paints and paintbrushes

Approach

1. Show the children Giacomo Balla's *Street Light*. Discuss Balla's technique of portraying the radiating light, and the colours he used to achieve this effect.

2. Ask the children to use coloured crayons on black card to experiment drawing fragments of light on a dark evening.

3. Demonstrate how the children can transfer their final design onto silk. Using the silk paints and brushes, start in the middle of the material and work outwards.

Umberto Boccioni

Umberto Boccioni (1882–1916) was a sculptor as well as a painter. His bronze sculpture *Unique Forms of Continuity in Space* is one of his most impressive works, vividly expressing bodily movements. He was born in Calabria, Italy, and in 1899 moved to Rome where he worked as a commercial artist. He experimented with various artistic styles, but it was only after he joined the Futurist movement in 1909 that his work became popular.

Approach

1. Show the children pictures of Boccioni sculptures and discuss what type of movement is portrayed. How does Boccioni depict power and movement?

2. Ask the children to sketch out a moving figure. Demonstrate where the weight would fall in the movement and how the arms and legs would be positioned.

3. Encourage the children to refer to their sketches as they try to interpret these movement ideas in a three-dimensional form, using pieces of cardboard and boxes.

4. Ask the children to glue the pieces of their sculpture together and spray them bronze.

Resources
- Pictures of sculptures by Umberto Boccioni
- Paper and pencils
- Cardboard modelling materials
- Boxes
- Glue
- Bronze spray paint

Vorticism was a short-lived British art movement founded by the painter and writer Wyndham Lewis (1882–1957). This genuinely avant-garde movement had its own identifiable form of geometric abstraction and its own vibrant and aggressive magazine called *Blast*. The magazine contained the movement's manifesto but there were only ever two publications of it. Vorticism was a movement that aimed to convey the noise and chaos of modern life, and was a spin-off from Futurism. Vorticist artists were fascinated with the machinery and industrial forms of the modern era. Despite great efforts to maintain the movement's momentum during World War I, it could not be sustained as most of its leading figures were in the services or working as war artists.

David Bomberg

David Bomberg (1890–1957) is often associated with Vorticism, a movement which shared the Cubist tendency towards abstraction and the Futurist interest in movement. He was born in Birmingham in 1890 but grew up in London. In 1908 he gave up an apprenticeship as a lithographer to devote himself to painting.

The Mud Bath, 1914 by David Bomberg (1890–1957) © Tate, London 2006.

Mud Bath Display

Resources
- Pictures of *The Mud Bath* by David Bomberg
- Paper and pencils
- Air-hardening clay
- White and blue paint
- Red card

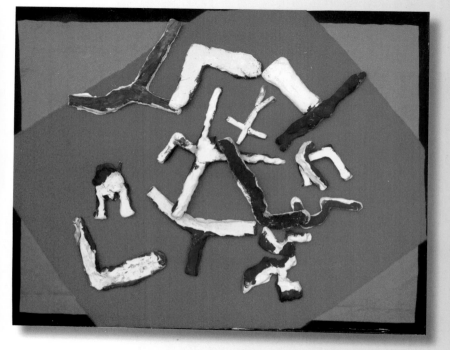

Approach

1. Show the children *The Mud Bath* by David Bomberg. Explain how it was based on sketches made at public baths in the Whitechapel area of London's East End where Bomberg grew up. The jagged semi-abstract shapes and energy depict the sort of images the Vorticists were aiming to achieve.

2. Ask the children to sketch out a figure bathing, swimming or just sitting, simplifying its form to geometric essentials.

3. Use clay to recreate the sketched figures in three-dimensional form. Allow the figures to dry.

4. Once dry, paint the figures, mirroring the blue and white of Bomberg's work.

5. Ask the children to display their models, with the emphasis on movement and chaos, on a background of red card.

In the Hold

Resources
- Picture of *In the Hold* by David Bomberg
- Wax pastels
- Pencils and rulers
- Cartridge paper, cut into large squares

Approach

1. Study a copy of David Bomberg's *In the Hold* picture.

2. Explain Bomberg's technique of representing images on a squared grid. The grid fragments the figures and turns a representational scene into a geometric pattern.

3. *In the Hold* was inspired by watching a group of workers moving passengers aboard a ship. It is a celebration of their strength and dignity, but by portraying their figures on a grid it implies that they are being taken over by the forces of mechanisation.

4. Ask the children to look at a small piece of the grid pattern and enlarge it by copying it onto a piece of square cartridge paper. Once they have completed a pencil sketch, they should choose colours that match the original.

5. Re-assemble each part of the grid to recreate the original picture.

Edward Wadsworth

Edward Wadsworth (1889–1949) was one of the most important English artists during the first half of the twentieth century. He studied at the Slade School of Fine Art and became a leading figure in the Vorticist movement. Wadsworth concentrated on industrial (particularly maritime) and still life subjects and worked in numerous mediums.

Vorticist Alphabet

Approach

1. Show the children pictures of the Vorticist alphabet designed by Wadsworth. Explain and discuss how the letters are embellished with a series of Vorticist compositions, some portraying groups of faceless robots and instruments of war.

2. Give each child a different letter of the alphabet to embellish with a Vorticist design. Encourage them to sketch out their ideas and then transfer their final design onto paper with black ink and felt pens.

Resources
- Pictures of Wadsworth's *Vorticist Alphabet*, c.1919
- Pictures of Vorticist artwork
- Cartridge paper
- Black ink and felt pens

Roofscapes

Approach

1. Look at the landscape Vorticist woodcuts by Edward Wadsworth. A lot of his work depicts industrial scenes from the north of England.

2. Ask the children to first sketch out an industrial scene and then use a mixture of media (card, ink, paint, and so on) to recreate a Vorticist woodcut-style picture of an industrial roofscape.

Resources
- Corrugated card
- Paper and pencils
- Pen and ink
- Paintbrushes

Abstract Art

There is no one simple and agreed definition of Abstract art. Usually the term means art that does not attempt to imitate or directly represent reality (although the work originally derived from an observation of reality). The history of Abstract art includes many modes of abstraction with different intentions and effects. It is generally claimed that the first Abstract painting was a watercolour painted in 1910 by Vassily Kandinsky. Although most Abstract art does not depict visible reality, Abstract artists have been inspired and have learnt from the diversities of decorative art, folk art, architecture, mathematics and geometry. Some paintings contain Abstract elements alongside figurative ones.

Abstract art has developed into many different movements and 'isms' and is now commonly regarded as the most characteristic form of twentieth-century art.

Fragment II for Composition VII, 1913 by Vassily Kandinsky (1866–1944) Image © Albright-Knox Art Gallery/ CORBIS; Artwork © ADAGP, Paris and DACS, London 2006.

Vassily Kandinsky

Vassily Kandinsky (1866–1944) was one of the great pioneers of Abstract painting. He was born in Odessa, Russia and first studied law and economics before taking up painting at the age of 30. He believed that Abstract art could set the soul vibrating, associating colours with musical notes and originally called his Abstract paintings 'colour music'. Kandinsky felt that every colour was like an emotion or a feeling – they could be angry, happy, strong or sad – and is quoted as saying that 'colour is the keyboard, the eyes hammers and the soul is a piano with many strings'.

Kandinsky Display

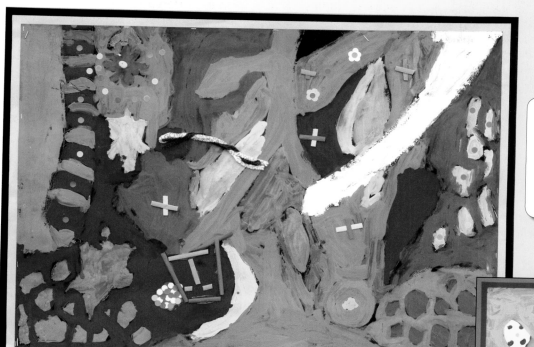

Resources
- Examples of Kandinsky's Abstract art
- Selection of music
- Paper
- Paint and paintbrushes

Approach

1. Listen to a selection of music, from popular to classical. Discuss the general differences between the styles of music and the techniques musicians use to affect our emotions.

2. Look at the picture *Fragment II for Composition VII* by Vassily Kandinsky on page 28 and discuss his colour code, for example red gave 'the impression of a strong drum beat' and yellow sounded 'like a high pitched trumpet'. Explore the children's own ideas as to which colours can be linked which musical sounds.

3. Look at other works by Kandinsky and talk about what sort of feelings they evoke and the music they could portray. Discuss what shapes could be linked to different musical sounds.

4. Together with the group, choose a piece of music that the children feel strongly affects their mood. Ask them to paint in the style of Kandinsky, choosing colours and shapes to visually interpret the music.

Piet Mondrian

Piet Mondrian (1872–1944) was born in Amersfoort, the Netherlands. His early paintings were realistic but he later became one of three key figures in the development of total abstraction, matched only in importance by Vassily Kandinsky and Kasimir Malevich. For Mondrian, the pure colours and straight horizontal and vertical lines of his Abstract paintings were an expression of the absolute harmony of the universe. He built his pictures from the simplest elements, with primary colours and straight lines forming squares and rectangles which he moved around the canvas until he found the perfect compositional balance. In 1940 Mondrian moved to New York where he died in 1944.

Cushion Covers

Resources
- Examples of work by Mondrian (*Composition with Red, Yellow and Blue*, 1921)
- Red, blue and yellow paper
- White cartridge paper
- Strips of black card
- Red, blue, yellow and black paint and paintbrushes
- Rulers
- Pencils
- Fabric
- Fabric paint
- Cushion pads

Approach

1. Encourage the children to engage with the pictures of Mondrian's work by asking questions such as: Does this painting represent anything? If so, what could it be? Why do you think he only used three primary colours? How do you think Mondrian composed his work? Is there anything to indicate the size of the painting?

2. Explain that all of Mondrian's paintings are based on the same principles, but the ratios of colour and the proportions of shape vary. Provide the children with some red, blue and yellow paper, a sheet of white cartridge paper and some strips of black card. Demonstrate how the children can explore different compositions by cutting up the paper into different sizes and laying down the strips of card in different places.

3. When the children have a composition they are happy with, ask them to transfer their design onto a piece of white fabric using a pencil and ruler.

4. Paint their pencilled design with fabric paints and wait for them to dry. Alternatively, the children can paint their design onto paper.

5. Make the painted designs into cushion covers or other textile products.

Georgia O'Keefe

Georgia O'Keeffe (1887–1986) was born in Sun Prairie, Wisconsin, USA. She studied art in Chicago and New York and worked first as a commercial artist and then as a teacher, which she gave up in 1918 to become a full-time artist. Georgia O'Keefe is often known for her paintings of mountains, bones and flowers. Her work moved between representation and abstraction and she was influenced by the ideas of Kandinsky. O'Keefe's career took off after some abstract drawings were shown to the influential photographer Alfred Stiglitz, whom she later married. She died in 1986 at the age of 99, and is arguably the best-known and the most committed woman artist in America.

Resources
- Examples of paintings by Georgia O'Keefe (e.g. *Oriental Poppies*, 1928)
- Viewfinders
- Pencils and paper
- Paint and paintbrushes

Flowers

Approach

1. Look at pictures by O'Keefe and discuss how the subject of her work is often seen from an extreme close-up, a point of view she borrowed from contemporary photography, which also concentrated on close examination of its subject. Ask the children to describe the painting's mood, looking at the colours. Ask: How does the painting make you feel? Does the close-up image abstract the flower too much? What do the shapes and forms remind you of?

2. Using a viewfinder, ask the children to isolate an area of the painting they particularly like.

3. Copy that area onto a sheet of cartridge paper, enlarging and abstracting the flower image even further.

4. Paint the enlarged image, encouraging the children to use blends and contrasts of colour in their work.

Surrealism

Surrealism was launched in Paris in 1924 as a 'shock treatment' for the art world. Surrealism means 'beyond the real' and at first it was a movement created largely by poets and writers who wanted to break away from the traditional art forms. Some Surrealist artists produced work which expressed experiences beyond their conscious control, others based their work on dreams they had experienced themselves. Surrealists were interested in memory, madness, chance and coincidence and loved anything magical, unusual, surprising or bizarre.

Man Ray

Man Ray (1890–1976) was an American photographer who became part of the Surrealist movement in Paris. He invented the photographic technique called Rayographs, which are abstract pictures made by arranging objects on a sheet of light-sensitive paper and exposing the paper to light.

Glass Tears by Man Ray (1890–1976) © Man Ray Trust/ADAGP 2006.

Resources

- Photographic paper
- Small items to put on the paper (leaves, scissors, pencils, and so on)
- Tray of fixer
- Tray of water
- Newspaper
- Tongs

Rayographs

Approach

1. Explain to the children what a Rayograph is and the unique qualities of photographic paper. The chemicals used are quite safe, but warn the children to use them carefully and avoid getting fixer on their hands or near their eyes.

2. Show the children how to remove a piece of photographic paper from the black bag and, working quickly, arrange small objects in an imaginative way on top of the paper.

3. Leave the paper and objects in the sunshine until the paper turns a deep colour. This could take anything from a few minutes to half an hour depending on the strength of the sun.

4. After exposure, remove the items and put the photographic paper into the tray of fixer for two minutes.

5. Remove with tongs and put the paper in a tray of water for five minutes. Lay the Rayograph on newspaper to dry.

Glass Tears

Resources
- Mirrors (one per child)
- Paper
- Art pencils
- Glass beads
- Glue

Approach

1. *Glass Tears* is one of Man Ray's most famous photographs. Show the picture on page 32 to the children and study the expression on the woman's face. Ask: Why did Man Ray choose only to feature the eyes in his photograph? Is the picture a convincing image of a woman crying?

2. Give the children a small mirror each and ask them to express different emotions: happiness, surprise, sadness, and so on. Encourage them to study what happens to the shape of the eyes and eyebrows.

3. Using Man Ray's approach of focusing on a small part of the face, ask the children to draw an expressionless picture of their eyes.

4. Glue the glass beads onto their sketches. Ask the children if the addition of the tears changes the emotion of their picture and how the study of the eyes could be changed to project a happy image.

5. Display the pictures together as a collage of a giant eye, with large tears and paper-sculpted eyelashes.

Surrealist Masks

Resources
- Examples of Surrealist pictures of faces
- Pencils and paper
- Plastic masks (one per child)
- Collage materials
- Paint and paintbrushes
- Glue

Approach

1. Show the children the example pictures and encourage them to study the faces. Often the images have a disturbing effect and many of the Surrealist faces look sinister and strange. Ask the children to collect and sketch their own ideas for a Surrealist face using these pictures for inspiration.

2. Give each child a plastic mask, provide a collection of collage materials and paint, and ask the children to transfer their ideas into the three-dimensional form.

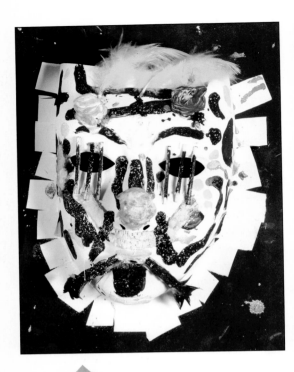

Joan Miró

Joan Miró (1893–1983) was born in Barcelona, Spain, the son of a goldsmith. He spent most of his working life in Paris, Barcelona and Majorca. Miró was one of the few Surrealists whose work tended towards abstraction, and his paintings were full of bizarre shapes, fantastic animals and strange insects. He believed in the power of the imagination and the unconscious mind and was referred to by Andre Breton as 'the most Surrealist of us all'.

Collage Eyes

Resources
- Examples of paintings by Joan Miró (e.g. *The Hunter (Catalan Landscape)*, 1923–24)
- Coloured paper
- Art straws
- Glue
- Scissors

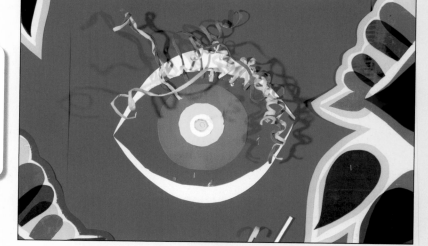

Approach

1. Eyes are an important symbol in Surrealist art; Dali painted a gigantic eye with a clock as its pupil. A lot of Miró's work from this period included images of eyes, often showing no emotion. Ask the children to look through copies of Miró's paintings and pick out pictures of eyes.

2. Demonstrate how to simplify and exaggerate the details of eyes and provide the children with a selection of coloured paper and art straws.

3. Use Miró's work as inspiration to create paper collages of eyes, incorporating paper-sculpting techniques of folding, curling, and so on.

Silk Screen Eyes

Resources
- Examples of paintings by Joan Miró (e.g. *The Hunter (Catalan Landscape)*, 1923–24)
- Paper and pencils
- Scissors
- Silk screens
- Squeegees
- Paint

Approach

1. As a small group project, look at some of the features of Miró's paintings of eyes. His work is often made up of bright geometric shapes. Encourage the children to develop a design that would not look out of place within a Miró painting. Explain that they will need to limit their use of colours to a maximum of three.

2. Prepare stencils for screen printing by photocopying each child's design; three copies for three colours, two copies for two colours, and so on.

3. Cut out the photocopied stencil for each colour.

4. Place the first stencil on the fabric and place the screen on top. Use a squeegee to pull the paint evenly from the top to the bottom. Allow to dry.

5. Repeat the process with the other stencils until the design is complete.

Guernica

War Art is concerned with subjects that have been affected by war, or caused by war, or sustain war.

From 1936 to 1939 there was a civil war in Pablo Picasso's native country, Spain. Guernica is a town in the Basque region which was bombed heavily in 1937. The town was totally destroyed and people who tried to escape were gunned down in the fields. Picasso was horrified – he hated war and violence in any form and believed the bombing was a despicable act. He was spurred into action straight away and began work on a huge canvas about the suffering of the innocent victims of the war. The resulting artwork, *Guernica*, is an enormous painting and measures roughly 3.5m by 7.5m. It is not an easy painting to understand, as Picasso deliberately distorted and exaggerated those parts of the body which express fear; the picture also includes many of his personal ideas and symbols.

Guernica Display

Approach

1. Show *Guernica* to the children and explain the historical facts behind the painting.

2. Talk about the images. Discuss how the humans (mainly women and children) and animals are mixed together. Ask: Why do you think Picasso did this? What effect does it have?

3. Ask the children to use a viewfinder to focus on one or two parts of the picture. Explain that this will help them to isolate particular images from what is a scene of great confusion. Encourage the children to study the distortions of their small area of the painting and try to identify what Picasso has portrayed.

4. Demonstrate, using a mixture of paint and card relief, how the children can reproduce their small part of the painting. Display the relief pictures together, recreating a composition similar to war-torn *Guernica*.

Resources
- Picture of *Guernica* by Pablo Picasso
- Viewfinders
- Paper and card
- Black and white paint

Paul Nash

Paul Nash (1889–1946) was an official war artist in both World Wars. He was a painter, watercolourist, printmaker, book illustrator and art critic. He was born in London, the son of a barrister and studied briefly at the London Slade School of Art. Nash was a landscape painter of considerable imaginative and poetic power. His career was varied and distinguished but many critics think that his World War I paintings mark the summit of his achievement.

Resources
- Examples of war prints by Paul Nash
- Cartridge paper
- Pencils
- Scissors
- Card
- Silk screens and squeegees
- Black paint

War Scene Silk Screen

Approach

1. Show the children pictures of Paul Nash war paintings and prints. Discuss how the jagged patterns of lines increase the nightmare effect of burnt out trees, mud and rubble.

2. Ask the children to sketch out a simple line drawing of a war scene in the style of Paul Nash.

3. Show them how to prepare a stencil by cutting out the main shapes of their war scene (for example, the trees) and discarding the cut out area.

4. Demonstrate how to place the stencil onto a sheet of card and lower the silk screen on top. Apply black paint along the top edge of the silk screen and use a squeegee to pull the paint evenly from the top of the screen to the bottom. Even application may require two or three pulls.

5. Remove the screen; the paper stencils will stick to the screen. Carefully remove the paper stencil to reveal the printed image.

Max Ernst

Max Ernst (1891–1976) was a German-born printer, printmaker, collagist and sculptor. He was born near Cologne and studied philosophy and psychology at Bonn University but abandoned his studies in 1911 to become a printer. He is credited with the invention of Surrealist painting. The imagery in his work is striking, thought-provoking and sometimes inexplicable. He invented the technique of 'frottage' (rubbing) and 'decalomania' (see below). He believed that by using less traditional methods of painting he could access his imagination and unconscious feelings more easily.

Decalomania

Resources
- Picture of *Europe After the Rain II* by Max Ernst
- Polystyrene sheets
- Thick paint
- Paper

Approach

1. Show the children the picture of *Europe After the Rain II* by Max Ernst. Ernst painted this picture in 1940–42, which were difficult years for him. He was horrified by the Spanish Civil War and World War II. Ernst painted this picture just before fleeing to America and it shows a horrific war-torn landscape. Discuss what the children can see in this picture.

2. Explain the technique of decalomania. This is a method of creating texture in paint which can then be worked into to create interesting images. Demonstrate the process by spreading paint thickly onto a surface (such as a polystyrene sheet) cut into an interesting shape. Press a sheet of paper down onto the textured paint and remove, leaving a furry, textured printed shape. Ask the children what their shapes remind them of, encouraging them to let their imaginations run wild. Explain that Ernst was a Surrealist and used this technique a lot in his paintings.

3. Give the children an opportunity to experiment with this technique to create their own war-torn landscape in the style of Ernst. Discuss how the gloomy landscape is contrasted against the bright blue sky.

Wyndham Lewis

Wyndham Lewis (1882–1957) was born on a yacht off Nova Scotia, Canada and came to England as a child. He studied at the Slade School of Art and became one of the leading Vorticist artists before World War I, editing the journal *Blast*. He served with the Royal Artillery and became an official war artist.

Blast Display

Resources
- Examples of *Blast* front covers
- Art pencils
- Paper
- Black, grey and white paint
- Paintbrushes

Approach

1. Explain to the children there were only ever two issues of *Blast*, the first in July 1914, the second in July 1915, a month after the one and only Vorticist exhibition. The Vorticists were a British group, a spin-off from Cubism and Futurism, but the outbreak of war quickly put an end to their activities.

2. Look at the images on the front cover of *Blast 2 – War Number*. Lewis wrote, 'A machine is in greater or less degree a living thing. Its lines and masses imply force and action.' Put this quote into context by discussing the fast-changing world in which the Vorticists lived. Talk about the feelings of aggression inherent in the work of the Vorticist artists and whether the anticipated war contributed to this aggression.

3. Much of Vorticist work expressed in non-representational terms thoughts of energy, force and mechanics. Encourage the children to focus on these concepts and sketch out images of mechanical violence in the style of *Blast* magazine.

4. Put individual sketches together and produce large pictures combining the work of several children.

5. Paint the large pictures in shades of black, grey and white.

Abstract Expressionism

Number 22, 1949 by Jackson Pollock (1912–56) Image © Christie's Images/CORBIS; Artwork © Pollock-Krasner Foundation/Artists Rights Society (ARS), New York and DACS, London 2006.

Abstract Expressionism was the name for an artistic movement that emerged in the USA during the 1950s. The artists within the movement produced large-scale dramatic Abstract paintings. There were two main types: 'action painting' and the quieter 'colour field painting'.

Action painting involved the use of spontaneous physical movement and gestures to produce artwork. Jackson Pollock became famous for his 'drip' paintings. Pollock used a revolutionary new technique, which involved dripping, pouring or squirting the paint from syringes directly onto the canvas. We now use the term action painting in a wider sense to refer to any technique of making a painting with energetic and spontaneous application of paint.

Other artists who also fall under the title of Abstract Expressionist include Mark Rothko, Barnett Newman and Clyfford Still. These artists invented a softer, calmer technique (colour field painting) where paint is applied with brushes in large areas or 'fields' of colour. There is often no frame or edge to the painting and the expanse of colour covers the whole surface.

Size was important to all Abstract Expressionists and many of their paintings were bigger than large windows; some were wall-sized and they were all meant to be viewed close-up.

Jackson Pollock

Jackson Pollock (1912–56) was born in Cody, Wyoming, USA. He was arguably the most important pioneer of Abstract Expressionism. He was one of a number of artists in America who experimented with radically new ways of painting and invented his 'drip' paintings in around 1947. Pollock became famous in 1949, when an issue of *Life* magazine asked, 'Is he the greatest living painter in the United States?' In 1941 he met his future wife, the artist Lee Krasner, whose career took off at a time when Pollock himself was becoming increasingly depressed and dependent on alcohol. He died in a car crash in 1956.

Drip Painting

Resources
- Examples of drip paintings by Jackson Pollock
- Large pieces of card
- Paint

Approach

1. Explain the process of drip painting, where paint is poured, dripped or splashed onto the canvas. Pollock did not use any brushes and, although the paint looks as if it has decided where to fall, Pollock carefully controlled the flow of the paint by his arm movements and general position. Stress to the children that it is an extremely controlled process and demonstrate how it can be achieved. Look at the picture of *Number 22* by Jackson Pollock on page 40 and encourage the children to try to absorb what the painting has to offer by asking questions such as: What is the title? Does the title evoke any images and feelings? Are these feelings reflected in the painting? What does it mean?

2. Encourage the children to think of a new title for a composition or choose one of Pollock's to recreate.

3. Ask the children to produce a semi-controlled composition in the style of Pollock, using the drip and splash technique. They could incorporate handprints or footprints, leaving a record of themselves in the painting.

Lee Krasner

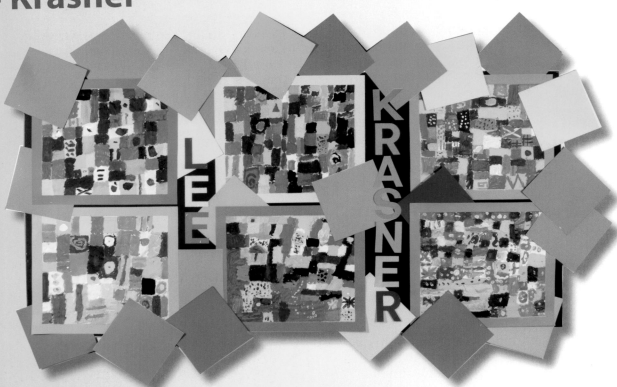

Lee Krasner (1908–84) was born in 1908 in Brooklyn, New York, USA, into a family of Russian-Jewish immigrants. She went to the only high school in New York that taught art to girls and nurtured an ambition to become an artist. By 1941 Krasner was gaining a reputation as an up-and-coming artist, but after meeting Jackson Pollock much of her life was devoted to helping promote his work; her own art never really took off until after his death in 1956.

Fabric Designs

Approach

Resources
- Examples of pattern work by Lee Krasner
- Pencils and paper
- Pieces of white calico fabric
- Fabric paint

1. Show the children pictures of Krasner's rectangular-patterned work.

2. Talk about the possible methods of creating a similar pattern. Discuss how the work has a feeling of balance about it. Ask: Can you estimate how many rectangles make up the design? Do you think they have been measured or randomly drawn? The fact that the pictures are often untitled suggests that they are purely patterns for their own sake. Look at the colours that have been used and the patterns within the rectangles and discuss how and why these have been chosen.

3. Demonstrate how to sketch out a similar patterned design and, once the children have experimented on paper, transfer their ideas onto fabric. Paint the patterns with brightly coloured fabric paint.

Mark Rothko

Mark Rothko (1903–70) was born in Dvinsk, Latvia into a Jewish family. When Rothko was ten, his family emigrated, settling in Portland, Oregon, USA. He went to Yale University but left after two years and headed for New York where he later enrolled to study art at the Art Students League. As an Abstract Expressionist he believed that Abstract art should reach deep levels of feelings.

Colour Field Painting in Pastel

Resources
- Examples of colour field paintings by Mark Rothko
- Chalk pastels
- Cotton wool
- Cartridge paper
- Scrap paper

Approach

1. Encourage the children to engage with the paintings by showing them several different pictures and asking how they feel when they look at them. Choose one that makes the children feel peaceful and one that affects their mood in a more negative way. Ask: Why have you responded in this way? What effects do the colours have in creating the mood?

2. Ask the children to choose an emotion to portray in the style of Rothko in chalk pastels and encourage them to think of two or three colours to complement each other to create this mood. Experiment with the colours and discuss how each one affects the one besides it. Consider the proportions of the coloured rectangles.

3. Collect dust from the chosen coloured chalk pastels by rubbing firmly onto a piece of scrap paper.

4. Use a piece of cotton wool to collect the dust and 'paint' onto the paper. Repeat with each colour.

5. When the children have finished, display the work and discuss whether they think the colour combinations have been successful in creating the chosen mood.

Colour Field Paintings in Ink

Resources
- White paper napkins
- Cartridge paper
- Coloured ink
- Paintbrushes
- Glue
- Paper

Approach

1. Follow the approach of the pastel colour field painting activity. Allow time to experiment with the coloured ink on the paper napkins; the thin paper becomes very fragile when wet and the coloured inks will seep into each other, creating fuzzy edges and secondary colours.

2. When the children have chosen their feelings and colours for their artwork, use glue to stick the paper napkins down on cartridge paper and paint with coloured ink.

3. Discuss the contrast between the pastel colour field paintings and the vivid colourful ink versions.

'A prudent art, what a stupid idea! Art is a compound of intoxication and madness.' (Jean Dubuffet, 1945). The term Art Brut (French for raw or rough art) was coined by Jean Dubuffet in the mid 1940s. Art Brut was produced by those outside the established art scene and Dubuffet believed that there was more truth in the unspoilt creative art of the untrained amateur than that of the professional artist. Dubuffet believed that the creator of Art Brut was not an artist (their creations were called 'works' rather than masterpieces) that they should be self-taught and defined them as 'persons estranged from culture who have not been informed or influenced by it'.

Jean Dubuffet

Jean Dubuffet (1901–85) was a Frenchman. He tried to reinvent art by looking at the world with childlike simplicity, uncluttered by history or tradition. He was often mocked by the public and art critics. From 1962–74 Dubuffet produced a series of works called *L'Hourloupe*. Whilst talking on the telephone he started doodling with a biro on some bits of paper. When he had finished talking he looked at the figures and shapes that he had accidentally created and then filled them with red and blue parallel ball point stripes. Dubuffet then cut out these figures and forms and realised that their appearance and effects changed as soon as he stuck them down onto a black background. He was very excited by what to him appeared to be the near-magic effect of the resulting imagery and made a little book of his pictures, which he called *L'Hourloupe*.

L'Hourloupe Display

Resources
- Examples of paintings from the *L'Hourloupe* collection by Jean Dubuffet
- White cartridge paper
- Felt pens
- Biros
- Black, red and blue card
- Glue

Approach

1. Show the children pictures of Jean Dubuffet's work from his *L'Hourloupe* collection. Explain how these designs were developed and created. Demonstrate how to doodle some shapes and ask the children to come up with some ideas of how to fill in the shapes and how to make an interesting pattern.

2. Give each child a piece of white cartridge paper and a selection of felt pens and encourage them to doodle without any preconception as to the final outcome of their design. Ask them to fill in the shapes to create a Dubuffet-style image.

3. Cut out some of the shapes and mount onto a mixture of red, blue and black card.

George Demkin

George Demkin was born in Russia and was a parachutist in Indochina before finding work as a mason in a Mediterranean town. He created Abstract works in gouache.

Demkin Display

Resources
- Examples of work by George Demkin (particularly *Composition with Eyes and Masks*, 1961)
- Viewfinders
- Cartridge paper and pencils
- Paint and paintbrushes

Approach

1. Look at examples of Art Brut, particularly the work of George Demkin. Explain to the children that the artists of this movement often looked to child art for fresh ways of seeing everyday things. They thought it was important to have a lack of artistic training and aimed for purity of expression and complete freedom to paint whatever they wanted.

2. Encourage the children to look at the compositions by George Demkin in terms of shapes, patterns and colours. Ask: What are the prominent patterns, shapes and colours? What effect does the busy, brightly coloured image have on the viewer? Can they find images of everyday objects in the composition?

3. Show the children how to use the viewfinders to highlight a particular area of interest in Demkin's work.

4. Demonstrate how to enlarge their selected area onto a piece of cartridge paper, adding any features or patterns that the children feel would enhance their picture.

5. Ask the children to paint their composition and give it a suitable title.

Pop art was one of the most influential twentieth-century art movements. It is often perceived as a celebration of western consumerism, a movement concerned with contemporary popular mass culture. It did not have a prescriptive programme but was a style of art that took into account, for the first time, how our modern world looks and the ways we receive information from it. Pop artists took images from advertising, movies, cartoons and the fast food industry. The pictures were blown up, distorted, repeated on grids and brightly coloured. In the USA the key figures of this artistic phenomenon were Roy Lichenstein, Claes Oldenburg and Andy Warhol. In Britain key figures included Peter Blake, David Hockney and Richard Hamilton, who famously listed the qualities of Pop art as '…popular, transient, expendable, low-cost, man-produced, young, sexy, gimmicky, glamorous and big business'.

Sgt Pepper's Lonely Hearts Club Band, 1967 by Peter Blake (1932–) © Apple Corps Ltd

Peter Blake

Peter Blake (1932–) was born in Dartford, Kent and started his artistic career at a very young age, going to art college when he was only 14 years old. Blake was a leading member of the British brand of Pop art. He usually worked in collage, adding popular artefacts such as magazine cuttings, cinema tickets and toys to his paintings. His work often included nostalgic images and decorations from lost or fading traditions, for example the circus or fairgrounds. Blake designed The Beatles' *Sgt Pepper's Lonely Hearts Club Band* album with his wife in 1967.

Sgt Pepper

Approach

1. Discuss musicians and groups of the 1960s. Explain that most western music is described as either classical or popular (pop). Play some tracks from *Sgt Pepper's Lonely Hearts Club Band* by The Beatles.

2. Explore the cultural revolution of the 1960s and how it encompassed the world of music, art, film, photography and fashion.

3. Collect and display images from the 1960s.

4. Look at the cover of *Sgt Pepper's Lonely Hearts Club Band* on page 46 and explain that the artist, Peter Blake, brought nostalgia to his work by incorporating pin-ups of the past, such as wrestlers and boxers, as well as pop and movie stars of the day. Discuss the way the collage has been put together using magazine cuttings and other images.

5. Give each child a copy of their photographic image and ask them to design hats, wigs, outfits and so on to stick onto the photograph.

6. Collect all the portrait collages together and reproduce the album cover.

Resources
- A copy of *Sgt Pepper's Lonely Hearts Club Band*
- An A4 digital photograph of each child
- A variety of collage materials
- Paint and paintbrushes
- Glue
- Scissors
- Large pieces of card to construct the collage on

7. Add other images to the collage: photographs of other people in the school community or famous people past and present.

Andy Warhol

Andy Warhol (1928–87) was born in Pittsburg, Pennsylvania, USA. He studied art in Pittsburg from 1945–49 and then worked as a commercial artist, winning the Art Director's Club Medal for his shoe advertisements in 1957. He was determined to break into the serious art world and by the 1960s Warhol was probably the most famous and controversial of all the Pop artists. He predicted that one day every individual would have 15 minutes of fame; he appeared obsessed with fame and was a brilliant self-publicist. Warhol called his studio 'The Factory', and from 1962 he stopped painting and began silk-screening his images instead. The images of his work were taken from the world of advertising, commerce and the media and most of his designs come in numerous versions of different sizes and colours.

T-shirt Designs

Approach

1. Look at the work of Andy Warhol. Explain that he was a painter, graphic artist and film-maker and a cult figure in the Pop art movement of the 1960s. In his early work, images of famous brands were repeated on a giant grid and looked as if they were on supermarket shelves or on a factory production line.

2. Ask the children to collect and choose famous cartoon images and experiment with simplifying them without losing the essence of the character.

3. When the children have chosen an image, draw and paint it in no more than three colours.

4. Photocopy the image three times and cut out a stencil for each colour.

5. Place the first stencil on a piece of white fabric and place the screen on top. Use a squeegee to pull paint evenly from the top of the screen to the bottom. Allow to dry.

6. Repeat the process with the other two stencils until the design is complete.

7. When dry, stick the design onto a cardboard cut-out of a T-shirt.

Resources
- Examples of work by Andy Warhol
- Paper and pencils
- Paint and paintbrushes
- White cotton fabric
- Silk screens
- Squeegees
- Card for mounting

Egg Display

Approach

1. Explain to the children that the egg paintings by Andy Warhol began as an Easter gift, but it was an idea he liked and expanded upon.

2. Show pictures of his work and demonstrate how he manipulated the egg images, making them smaller then larger until the egg became an abstract shape. He took many Polaroid pictures of eggs in his studio and the flash distorted the curve and shape of the egg. His work on eggs became part of an important group of work dealing with Warhol's own view on Abstract art.

3. Blow up balloons into egg shapes and then papier mâché them with several layers of paper. Allow to dry.

4. Use an egg-shaped template and encourage the children to experiment with designs for their papier mâché balloon 'eggs'.

Resources
- Examples of egg paintings by Andy Warhol
- Balloons
- Papier mâché glue
- Paper
- Pencils
- Paint and paintbrushes
- Card
- Coloured paper

5. Ask the children to recreate their designs in paint on coloured paper, card and their papier mâché eggs.

Roy Lichtenstein

Roy Lichtenstein (1923–1997) was born in New York City, USA and studied at Ohio State University. In the 1950s he worked as a freelance commercial and graphic artist before becoming a teacher. Lichtenstein was fascinated with comics and he wanted to exaggerate their fun energy and larger than life qualities in his art. He enlarged small pictures from comics into huge, wall-sized paintings; he liked the clear colourful images. Often Lichtenstein would recreate just one or two frames of a comic story and the images would therefore be out of context.

Cartoons

Resources
- Examples of work by Roy Lichenstein
- A variety of comics
- Viewfinders
- Card
- Pencils
- Acrylic paints and paintbrushes
- Black marker pen

Approach

1. Show the children work by Roy Lichenstein. Give them an opportunity to look through some comics and choose an image or frame that particularly appeals to them.

2. Demonstrate how to oversimplify the composition, perhaps using a viewfinder to highlight a specific part of the frame.

3. Ask them to draw their chosen image onto a large piece of card and paint the picture using acrylic paints, outlining in black marker pen.

Claes Oldenburg

Claes Oldenburg (1929–) was born in Sweden but emigrated with his family as a child, settling in Chicago. He decided to become an artist whilst studying at Yale University and in 1956 he moved permanently to New York. Oldenburg looked at everyday ordinary objects, such as clothes pegs and toothpaste tubes, and made them into giant sculptures. He also made large food structures stuffed with foam.

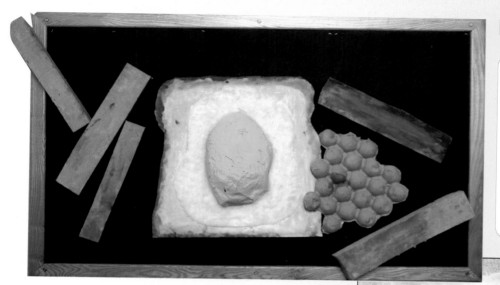

Food Structure

Resources

- Examples of food structures by Claes Oldenburg (e.g. *Floor Burger*, 1962; *Ice Cream Being Tasted*, 1964)
- Large pieces of foam
- Paint and paintbrushes
- Scissors
- Glue
- Card

Approach

1. Show the children pictures of Oldenburg food structures and discuss possible ways of recreating them. Give the children pictures of everyday packaged food and fast food products and ask them to choose some to turn into large structures.

2. Demonstrate how to cut large sheets of foam into the required shapes for the sculpture.

3. Mix appropriate coloured paint and paint accordingly.

4. To make the tube structure, design and paint the packaging on a large piece of card before rolling up and stapling together. Use polystyrene bowls for the bottom and the lid to make the structure firm.

Nataraja, 1993 by Bridget Riley (1931–) Image © Tate, London 2006; Artwork © 2006 Bridget Riley. All rights reserved.

Op art is a style of abstract painting which flourished in the late 1950s and 1960s and explored the effects of optical illusions. Op art is an abbreviation for 'Optical art' and relies completely on visual dynamics, or what might be described as 'quivering illusions of movement', for its effectiveness. Paintings were often made of sharply defined contrasting lines, and most Op artists worked out their geometrical images carefully in advance using scientific theories to make them appear to move. The viewer is left feeling that the image is constantly shifting and Op art actually evokes a physical response, not just an emotional one.

Op art became something of a craze in women's fashion in the 1960s and the two most famous exponents of Op art, Bridget Riley and Victor Vasarely, had a considerable impact on the world of textiles and design.

Bridget Riley

Bridget Riley (1931–) was one of the best known Op artists. She was born in London and studied at Goldsmith's College, London from 1949–53. She was originally inspired by Pointillism and her first paintings in the early 1960s were almost all in black and white. Riley began to reintroduce colour and her later work is a kaleidoscope of colours, meticulously arranged in thin diamond-shaped strips which create optical illusions. Riley does not paint every centimetre of the canvas herself and often assistants are employed to apply the acrylic paint, purely because it is practical. Riley's subject matter has been restricted to a simple but effective vocabulary of abstract shapes: squares, ovals, circles, lines, stripes and curves.

Geometric Designs

Resources
- Examples of work by Bridget Riley
- Large sheets of squared paper
- Pencils
- Rulers
- Paint and paintbrushes

Approach

1. Look at the example of Bridget Riley's work, *Nataraja*, on page 52. Discuss the shapes and colours and explore the children's visual response to it. Explain that she works out her preliminary designs on squared paper.

2. Demonstrate on a large piece of squared paper how the diamond shapes can be achieved by drawing vertical parallel lines at differing widths across the paper and joining them up diagonally.

3. Discuss the colours that Bridget Riley has used and how these contribute to the visual effect.

4. Choose three or four colours, then plan out which areas are going to be painted in each colour, then paint.

5. The children can work on individual pictures or a group composition.

Black and White Op Art

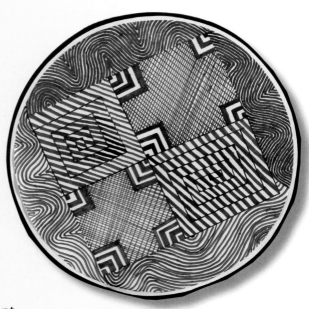

Resources

- Examples of black and white Op art (e.g. *Movement in Squares*, 1961 by Bridget Riley)
- Strips of black and white paper
- Black and white paper
- Art straws
- Black and white paint
- Compasses or circular templates
- Scissors
- Glue
- Black felt pens

Approach

1. Show the children examples of black and white Op art. Discuss what the Op artists were trying to achieve and comment on the effectiveness of each design.

2. Give the children the opportunity to experiment with cut strips of black and white paper to create a pattern. Encourage them to lay the stripes vertically, diagonally, horizontally, overlapping, and so on. Ask: What different effects can you create?

3. Use the same strips of paper and distort the stripes by cutting and folding to create new patterns.

4. Try arranging white art straws in geometric patterns that confuse the eye.

5. Introduce the idea of circles and squares into the design procedure. Alternate black and white circles and squares. Ask: What effect does this create? Ask the children to produce a black and white Op art design on the theme of violence and peace, turbulence and calmness. Encourage them to think about what shapes and mixture of lines they will choose.

6. When the children have had an opportunity to experiment, discuss and share their ideas. Ask them to roughly sketch their image onto a piece of paper. Explain that they will only be allowed black and white paper and paint to produce their final picture.

7. Display the various designs on a chequered background to reinforce the optical effects.

Vertical and Horizontal Relief Patterns

Resources
- Black and white paper
- Thin cardboard
- Glue
- Scissors

Approach

1. Demonstrate to the children how to roll up tubes of white paper in different dimensions and glue them in place. Allow to dry.

2. Arrange the white paper tubes onto a white background, varying the distance between each, and glue them firmly in place.

3. Show the children how to cut out strips of black paper in different thicknesses of wavy and straight lines. Experiment with arranging the black strips on the relief design.

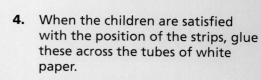

4. When the children are satisfied with the position of the strips, glue these across the tubes of white paper.

5. Display the designs on a background of relief wavy lines in various colours.

Kinetic Art

Kinetic art is art that moves, or appears to move, and the word 'kinetic' comes from the Greek word *kenesis*, which means movement. Kinetic sculptures can move electronically using motors, or more often just wind power. In addition to works employing actual movement, another form of Kinetic art relies on the spectator's movement for the illusion of movement and Op art paintings are sometimes included within the field of Kinetic art.

Fashion Bag Designs

Resources

- Examples of Op art by Victor Vasarely
- Commercially bought or handmade paper carrier bags
- Paint and paintbrushes
- Circular and square templates
- Pencils and rulers

Approach

1. Explain to the children that Op art (an abbreviation of 'Optical art') exploits certain optical phenomena to cause a painting to appear to vibrate or flicker. Op art became something of a craze in women's fashion, and one of Vasarely's designs was used on the plastic carrier bags of France's chain of co-op stores.

2. Show the children copies of Victor Vasarely's work. Explain that as a child he had been fascinated by grids, and in later life much of his Op art was based on optical grids. Most of his early works were in black and white, but his later ones were in colour where the combinations of different tones produces some subtle optical movements.

3. Ask the children to experiment with colours that stimulate an interesting visual glow. When the children have chosen their colours, map out a grid on the paper bag and use a square and circle template to recreate an Op art design.

4. Paint in chosen colours.

Alexander Calder

Alexander Calder (1898–1976) was the pioneer of Kinetic art or 'moving sculpture'. He was the son and grandson of sculptors. Some of his earliest pieces were motor-driven, but on the whole he relied on wind power. In the 1930s, influenced by artists Piet Mondrian and Joan Miró, he began to experiment with abstract painting and wire constructions; he once said that he wished to make 'moving Mondrians'. Many of his late works were huge, delicately balanced mobiles commissioned for public spaces.

Fish Mobiles

Resources
- Pictures of work by Piet Mondrian and Alexander Calder (e.g. *Brazilian Fish*, 1947 by Alexander Calder)
- Wire
- Wire cutters
- Scissors
- Card in primary colours, black and white

Approach

1. Look at the work by Piet Mondrian and Alexander Calder and discuss why Calder said he wished to make 'moving Mondrians'. Discuss whether the children can see the Mondrian influence in his mobiles.

2. Look at other mobiles by Calder and challenge the children to explore the concept of a moving sculpture and ask them to sketch out some ideas for a fish mobile, thinking about shapes and colours.

3. Demonstrate the technique for modelling a mobile using card and wire. Show the children how to join pieces of wire, glue card onto the wire and hang the mobile.

Minimalism and Conceptualism

Minimalism was an art movement formed in the 1950s, originating in America, and it flourishes to the present day. The Minimalists shared Piet Mondrian's belief that a work of art should be completely conceived in the mind before its execution. Minimalism focuses on space and form, using very simple shapes. It challenges the viewer to scrutinise the formal properties of what is actually there and see the world with fresh eyes. The work is usually rigorously geometric and involves the repetition of identical objects. Early minimalist work was predominantly three-dimensional and its three key sculptors were Dan Flavin, Carl Andre and Donald Judd. Painters who also embraced the idea of Minimalism include Frank Stella and Robert Ryman. The work produced by these artists is very important as it challenged what art could be made from, although to its critics Minimalist art seemed to show nothing much at all. Minimalist artists did not believe their work should grow organically but that it should be completely planned beforehand.

Carl Andre

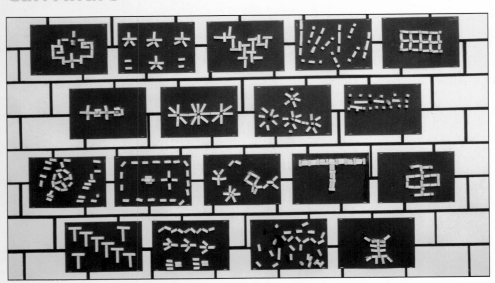

Carl Andre (1935–) is an American sculptor and poet. He was born in Quincy, Massachusetts, USA and is one of the best known exponents of Minimalism. He attended the Phillips Academy, Andover, USA where he became a close friend of fellow pupil Frank Stella. He is best known for producing sculptures of identical, ready-made commercial units in simple geometric arrangements. He also used three-dimensional natural products, such as hay bales and logs, in a sculpture of bricks in the Tate Gallery. The sculpture was vandalised and there was an outcry about the alleged waste of public money spent on its purchase.

Brick Sculptures

Approach

1. Show the children pictures of Carl Andre sculptures and discuss the theory of Minimalism.

2. Give the children the opportunity to discuss and plan their own small-scale brick sculpture on paper first. Encourage them to think about the shape and form of their construction.

3. Demonstrate how to safely saw the wood strips into identically sized bricks.

4. Ask the children to create their sculpture on the card, using their sketches as a guide. Once they are happy with their design, instruct the children to glue the bricks in position on the card.

Resources
- Pictures of Carl Andre sculptures (e.g. *Equivalent VIII*, 1966)
- Paper and pencils
- Strips of wood
- Saws
- Sawing blocks
- Glue
- Thick card

Frank Stella

Frank Stella (1936–) was born in Malden, Massachusetts, USA. The main thrust of his work was to emphasise the idea that a painting is a physical object: '…a flat surface with paint on it, nothing more … only what can be seen is there.' Stella became an influential figure in the development of Minimalism. In the 1960s he was one of several painters making pictures which seemed to be about nothing other than repeated patterns, painted in metallic or synthetic colours.

Geometric Display

Approach

1. Explain to the children the concept of Minimalist art. Discuss how it focuses on space and shape and has no hidden messages.

2. Look at the examples of Frank Stella's work with the children and discuss how the style could be achieved.

Resources
- Examples of geometric Minimalist work by Frank Stella (e.g. *Hyena Stomp*, 1962)
- Squared paper
- Rulers
- Paper and pencils
- Paint and paintbrushes

3. Invite the children to sketch their own Frank Stella design using a geometric grid on squared paper.

4. When they are happy with their design, ask the children to add paint to complete their picture. Cut out and group the pictures together as a geometric display.

Robert Ryman

Robert Ryman (1930–) was born in Nashville, Tennessee, USA. He is one of the foremost American abstract artists of his generation. He is regarded as a Minimalist painter and his works explore a myriad of surfaces and textures and are mainly white paintings.

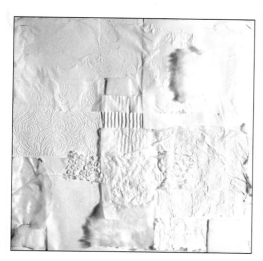

White Paintings

Approach

1. Show the children pictures by Robert Ryman. Explain that he was known as the painter of white paintings and that Ryman experimented with textures, synthetic or natural materials and delicate or tough surfaces.

2. Allow the children time to explore the texture of all the available materials and experiment with the effects of chalk pastel and thickness of paint.

3. Encourage the children to be adventurous and to produce a white painting in the style of Robert Ryman. Suggest music which could complement the work.

Resources
- Examples of white paintings by Robert Ryman
- Collection of white materials of different textures (including papers and materials)
- White paint
- Paintbrushes
- Chalk pastels
- Glue
- Scissors

Conceptual Art

Conceptual art was established in the late 1960s and 1970s as a development from Minimalist art. Members of this movement believe that the concept behind a work of art is more important than its physical expression. In Conceptual art, the idea is the most important aspect of the work and all planning and decisions are made beforehand. Conceptual artists explore ways of conveying these ideas without the use of traditional media and often use documents, photographs, statements, maps or even an action or event to present their concept. Some of these works appear deliberately banal while others set out to shock or amuse.

Richard Long

Richard Long (1945–) is a British artist whose work brings together sculpture, Conceptual art and Land art. Most of his art has been based on long, solitary walks where he makes sculptures using the basic elements of the natural world. He documents his walks with photographs which refer to things he passes. Sometimes he collects objects such as twigs and stones and arranges them into designs, usually simple geometric shapes.

Resources
- Examples of photographic work by Richard Long (from his book *A Walk Across England*, Thames and Hudson, 1997)
- Cameras and film or digital cameras
- Pen and paper

A Walk Across…

Approach

1. Show the children examples of work by Richard Long. Discuss how his style could be defined. Ask: Is it sculpture, Land art, Conceptual art, or all three? Why?

2. Focus on the Conceptual aspects of his work and explain that his thoughts are represented in the form of documentation; it is the idea or concept that is the most important aspect of the work, not the finished product. Look at the work of Richard Long again, particularly the photographs and narrative passages describing his walks around Britain. Discuss the concept or idea behind the photographic image and text; Conceptual art has a heavy reliance on language. Ask: What part does language play in Long's work?

3. If possible, take the children out for a walk, documenting photographically interesting objects and landmarks along the way. Encourage the children to write down their observations.

4. Back in the classroom, read some of the text passages that accompany Richard Long's photographs (see below) and ask the children to extend their observations into short texts. Develop these short texts into poems entitled 'A walk across… :

I went down to the sea to start
A walk across England as art
Along lanes past flowers
In sunshine and showers
Carrying a stone each day close to my heart.

Poem from *Richard Long: A Walk Across England* by Richard Long. © 1997 Richard Long. Reprinted by kind permission of Thames and Hudson Ltd., London.

Sol LeWitt

Sol LeWitt (1928–2007) is an American sculptor, writer and graphic artist who coined the term Conceptual art, which was established in the late 1960s as a development from Minimalism. He was born in Hartford, Connecticut, USA and studied fine art at Syracuse University, New York. As well as being a Conceptual artist he is regarded as one of the leading exponents of Minimalism.

Pattern Paintings

Resources
- Examples of paintings by Sol LeWitt
- Rulers
- Paint and paintbrushes
- Paper

Approach

1. Look at the paintings by Sol LeWitt with the children. Discuss the shapes, patterns and his use of colours.

2. Invite the children to work to a similar theme, to design and paint a pattern using bright primary and secondary colours.

Sol LeWitt Sculptures

Resources
- Pictures of sculptures by Sol LeWitt
- Pipe cleaners
- Paper straws

Approach

1. Explain to the children that Sol LeWitt structures characteristically involve combinations of simple basic elements. Show pictures of his work and discuss how they were made and the possible concept behind them.

2. Demonstrate how to use pipe cleaners to join paper straws together. Invite the children to work in small groups to collectively produce a structure in the style of Sol LeWitt.

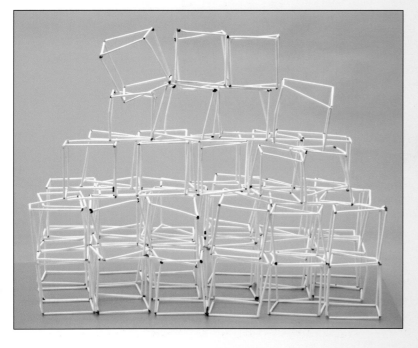

Land Art

Land art is a twentieth-century art movement that involves artists going out into the environment and making their mark on it. Artists work within the landscape creating simple arrangements of natural materials. Often these are only temporary and the only record that remains is photographic and paper documentation; the work is not made to endure. More recently, some Land artists have exhibited sculptures made from naturally 'found' objects inside galleries. Land art first appeared in the USA in the late 1960s. Part of its appeal is that, in many cases, the artist's work is changed or obliterated completely by the force of nature. Many artists welcome the ephemeral quality of Land art because it means their work cannot be owned; they aim to keep their art 'pure'.

Andy Goldsworthy and His Natural Sculptures, 1989 by Andy Goldsworthy (1956–) Image © Philippe Caron/Sygma/CORBIS; Artwork © Andy Goldsworthy

Andy Goldsworthy

Andy Goldsworthy (1956–) was born in Cheshire and now lives in Dumfriesshire, Scotland. He studied at Bradford College of Art and Preston Polytechnic. He works in specific locations creating pieces of art that interact with their setting, taking natural materials such as stones and leaves and arranging them into simple shapes. Goldsworthy is interested in movement, change, growth and decay and his work aims to heighten awareness of the beauty of nature.

Autumn Leaves

Resources
- Examples of leaf designs by Andy Goldsworthy (e.g. *Leaves with Hole*)
- Pictures of autumn trees and leaves
- Collage materials
- Paint and paintbrushes
- Scissors
- Glue

Approach

1. Show the children the leaf designs by Andy Goldsworthy. Discuss how he constructed the work and the practicalities of producing Land art in terms of natural materials, weather conditions, and so on.

2. If the season permits, collect brightly coloured autumn leaves and bring them into the classroom; if not, pictures will substitute. Allow the children the opportunity to explore their textures, colours, smells and shapes.

3. Using leaf templates, ask the children to imaginatively decorate an autumn leaf, mixing appropriate colours, and to embellish using a variety of collage materials.

4. Display in the form of an Andy Goldsworthy Land art composition.

Winter Twig Sculpture

Approach

1. Show the children the photographs of Land art. Explain that most Land art sculptures are made within the outside environment, but that some works are made and exhibited in galleries.

2. Demonstrate how to arrange a collection of twigs in an unusual shape, securing the arrangement with wire.

3. Spray the arrangement silver and sprinkle with glitter.

4. Encourage the children to use the sculpture creatively by taking it into the environment and photographing scenes through the 'window' of the sculpture.

Resources
- Photographs of Land sculptures
- Twigs
- Wire
- Can of silver spray and glitter

Stone Wall

Approach

1. Use the photographs to encourage the children to explore the range of shapes used to make dry stone walls. Ask them to observe the detail in tone, line, colour, surface, texture, and so on. Encourage them to build a vocabulary and an eye for the environment and the colours and patterns within it. Talk about how the stones reflect the light in different ways. Look at the spaces between the stones and discuss what is growing there.

2. Glue the photographs onto a small area on a large piece of card. Invite the children to copy and enlarge a section of the photographs to fill the card. Refer the children back to their observations and encourage them to use this information in their designs.

Resources
- Photographs of dry stone walls
- Large piece of card
- Glue
- Paint and paintbrushes
- Collage materials
- Scissors
- Crayons, felt pens, wax pencils
- Paper
- Leaf template

3. Ask the children to paint the wall, mixing colours carefully to match the photographs.

4. Give the children a leaf template to draw round and cut out.

5. Demonstrate the use of collage materials to add texture: moss, flowers, insects, and so on.

6. Ask the children to imaginatively recreate the vegetation, animals and insects that may lie under a fallen leaf in woodland. Provide a variety of materials to create their design.

7. Display all the separate elements together as a giant stone wall.

Tree Leaf Designs

Approach

1. The practical problems involved in getting large groups of children into the environment to plan and produce art means that a lot of preparatory work needs to be done in the classroom, through the use of photographs and photocopies. Take photographs of trees, then photocopy and stick each image on a larger sheet of cartridge paper. Give each child a copy.

2. Encourage the children to extend the tree picture, drawing ideas that could be used as a design sheet for a Land sculpture.

3. Ask the children to imagine they are going to create a piece of Land art using autumn leaves. Use felt examples of leaves and compose their sculpture on a large photocopy of a tree.

4. By planning art within the classroom in this format, the children will develop ideas for shaping the environment in the way that Land artists do and start to imaginatively compose ideas based on the studies they have done.

Resources
- Pictures of trees
- Cartridge paper
- Pencils
- Felt
- Felt glue

Sunflower Patterns

Resources
- Pictures of sunflowers
- Paper
- Paint and paintbrushes
- Withie canes
- Masking tape
- PVA glue
- Sponges
- Tissue paper

Approach

1. Look at pictures of sunflowers with the children and discuss their shapes and colours. Ask the children to draw a simple outline of a sunflower and to paint it in bright colours and patterns.

2. Soak the withie canes in water for an hour or so to make them more pliable. Demonstrate how to bend the canes into petal shapes and secure with masking tape.

3. Make a mix of PVA glue and water in a bowl and use a sponge to carefully cover a sheet of tissue paper with the glue.

4. Drape the tissue paper over the withie cane petal frame and cover with another layer of the PVA mixture so that the tissue paper dries hard.

5. Make a circular centre in the same way. Display with the children's painted sunflower pictures.

6. Ask the children to create a similar flower design using daisies or dandelions, if possible in their school environment.

Graffiti Art

Graffiti means 'little scratches' in Italian and although it dates back to ancient times it was only in the twentieth century that people began to think of it as art and not simply vandalism. Graffiti, in its modern meaning, describes anything scribbled or sprayed onto walls in a public space. The Graffiti movement was at its high point in the 1980s, being almost exclusively American rooted in the New York subway. Its key figures were Keith Haring and Jean Michel Basquiat. Graffiti art is also called Spraycan art and Subway art. Graffiti art was less in vogue in Britain.

Donut Revenge by Jean-Michel Basquiat (1960–88) Image © Christie's Images/ CORBIS; Artwork © ADAGP, Paris and DACS, London 2006.

Jean-Michel Basquiat

Jean-Michel Basquiat (1960–88) was born in Brooklyn, New York City, USA. His father was an accountant from Haiti and his mother was of Puerto Rican decent. His childhood was marked by his parent's separation and his school days were rebellious and difficult. Basquiat became part of a loosely associated group of so-called 'Graffiti artists' and his work first appeared on subway walls and often featured scrawled writing or symbols.

In Basquiat's short but highly productive eight- or nine-year career he created nearly 1000 original paintings and almost 2000 works on paper. He was especially sensitive to the racial prejudice and social injustice that confronts all minority groups and this is a theme which is a constant undercurrent in his work. He died tragically young at the age of 27, from a massive drug overdose.

Basquiat-Style Art

Resources

- Examples of work by Jean-Michel Basquiat (e.g. *Untitled*, 1981; *Future Science Versus Man*, 1983)
- Paper and pencils
- Cartridge paper
- Ink rollers
- Trays
- Coloured inks
- Wax pastels

Approach

1. Look at the picture of Basquiat's work, *Donut Revenge*, on page 68. Discuss the content of the images which Basquiat said were '…exploring the black experience'. Encourage them to consider what he was trying to convey. Basquiat painted awkward and rough observations of city life. Ask: Why did he put his art on the street and subway?

2. Ask the children to sketch out some Graffiti-style images of their observations of a fast-moving, chaotic city life. Suggest that they could include people at work, play or copy a particular part of Basquiat's work that captures their interest.

3. Demonstrate, using an ink roller and coloured ink, how to prepare a colour wash background on cartridge paper for their design. Allow to dry.

4. Invite the children to transfer their sketched images onto the colour wash background with wax pastel.

Keith Haring

Keith Haring (1958–90) was born in Reading, Pennsylvania, USA. Haring studied the visual arts and was taught drawing, sculpture, painting and art history at the School of Visual Arts in New York. Keith Haring first achieved notoriety in the early 1980s when he painted on the black paper hangings used for displaying advertising posters in the New York City subway. His rapidly executed drawings of line figures were created in plain white chalk. It was while he was in New York that he became friends with Basquiat. By 1984, he had brought his underground art up to street level and into some of the world's most prestigious museums. He was inspired by the hustle and bustle of life in a big city and felt the medium of Graffiti art spoke directly to the public in the language of the street. Like Basquiat, he felt he had to take painting and sculptures back from the academics and spectators and give it back to the people. Keith Haring died of AIDS in 1990. He was only 31 years old.

Chalk Pictures

Resources
- Examples of chalk pictures by Keith Haring
- Paper and pencils
- Black paper
- White chalk

Approach

1. Show the children examples of Keith Haring's black and white pictures. Haring's cartoon-like style is instantly recognisable. Explain that his first drawings were comic strips and that he had a talent for telling stories with pictures.

2. Ask the children to sketch out some simple cartoon shapes using examples of Keith Haring's work as inspiration.

3. Invite the children to transfer their designs onto black paper with white chalk.

Monkey Puzzle

Resources
- An example of a *Monkey Puzzle* work by Keith Haring
- Cartridge paper
- Pencils
- Paint

Approach

1. Discuss how the monkey-like figures in Keith Haring's work resemble the kind of images found on primitive wall paintings. They have a lot of energy and seem to be engaged in a dance. People often asked Keith Haring to explain what his drawings really meant, and he used to reply, 'It's your job to decide. I only do the paintings.' Encourage the children to engage with the paintings by asking: What are the monkeys doing? How are they moving? Is it a happy picture or sad?

2. Ask the children to draw a large monkey motif and paint it in a choice of two colours, using Haring's *Monkey Puzzle* as inspiration.

3. Other groups of children could work together to recreate a circular pattern of monkeys.

4. Display all of the finished designs on brightly coloured backing paper.

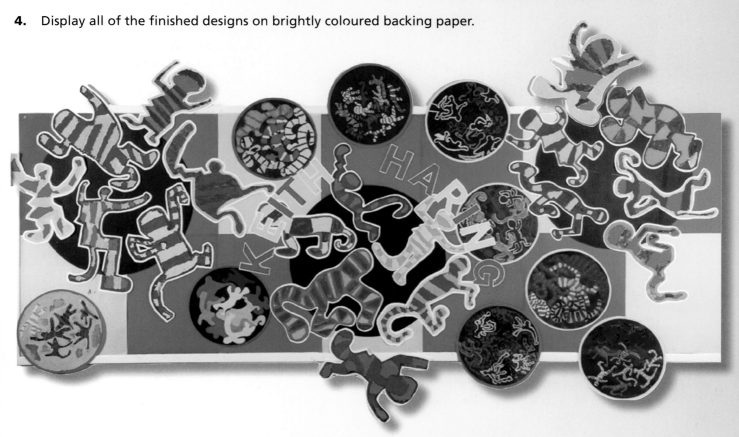

Geometric Display (page 59)